Sammy the Centipede Goes to the Chiropractor

by **Maria Luchsinger**

Illustrations by
Joe Palmisano

ISBN: 978-0-9897630-4-2

Printed in the U.S.A.

Sammy the Centipede Goes to the Chiropractor

by Maria Luchsinger

Illustrations by Joe Palmisano

Hi! I'm Sammy
the centipede,
and I am going to
tell you what it is
like to visit a
chiropractor.

I'm Sammy
the centipede,
I'm feeling very fine.
A visit to my
chiropractor
Keeps my spine in line.

I love to climb! One day, I was inching my way up my favorite tree. I had almost reached the place I wanted to be, but I had to stretch a little too far with my front legs.

Down I went and hit the ground with a thud!
I looked like a train that had gone off the track.
I straightened myself out and slowly stood up.
I was a little sore, but I thought I would be okay.

Later that day, I was riding my bicycle built for 15 pairs of legs. I was having a wonderful ride and enjoying the beautiful day. Suddenly, I tried to go around the corner too quick. I lost control of the steering, and my legs could not work the pedals.

I ended up in a heap.
Even though I was wearing a helmet,
I had a headache, my legs were sore,
and my stomach didn't feel too well either.

I knew this would be a good time to call my friend the chiropractor for an appointment. Even though taking medicine sometimes makes me feel better, it doesn't always take care of the real reason I'm not feeling well. My chiropractor will give me a checkup that is different from the one I get from other kinds of doctors. He will do a checkup of my spine.

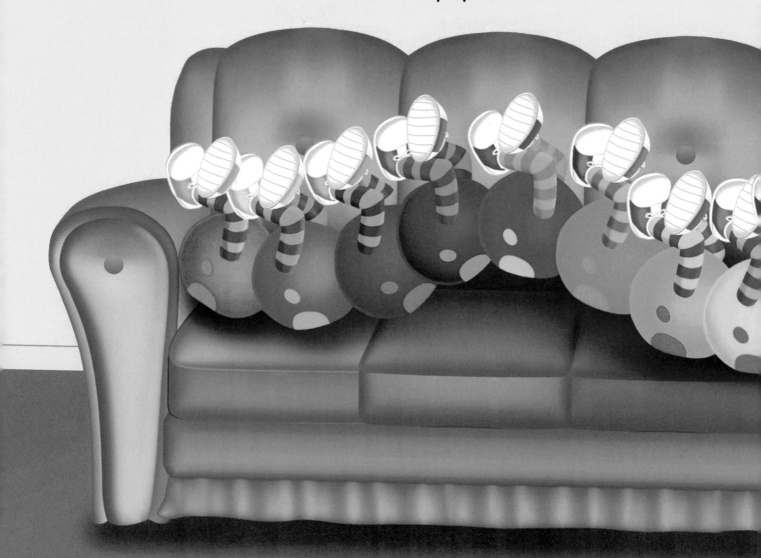

You have a spine that protects your nervous system. Your brain sends messages to different parts of your body using your nervous system. It works like a computer inside your body. The brain has helpers called the spinal cord and nerves.

There is a long string of bones inside you that starts at the top of your head and goes down your back to where you sit. This is called your spine.

You can feel the bumps with your hands if you put your hands in the middle of your back. All of these bones have to move and protect the nerves.

Each bone has a hole where the nerves pass through to the rest of your body. Can you see the different sections of my body? You have different sections of spinal bones that make up your spine.

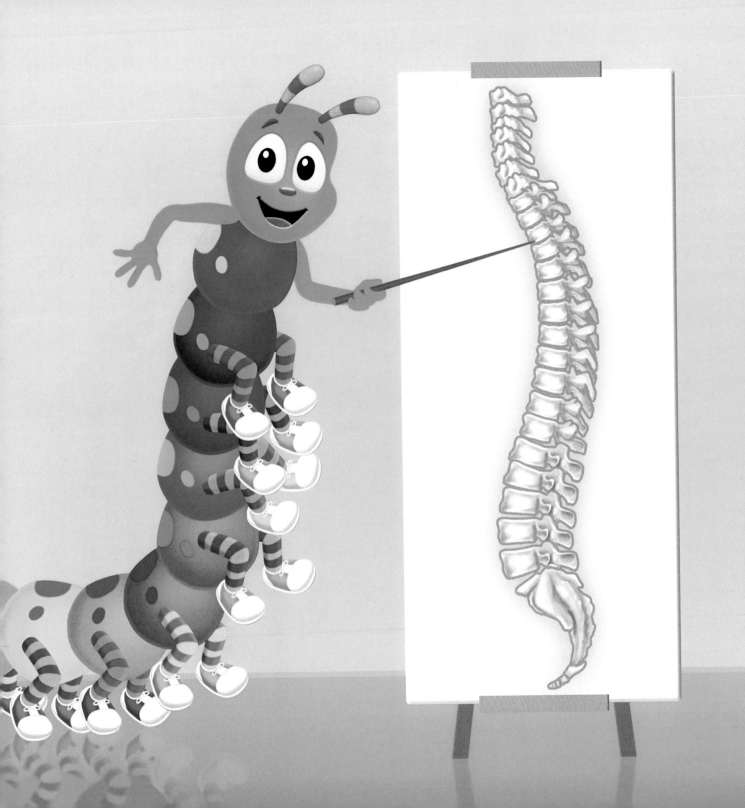

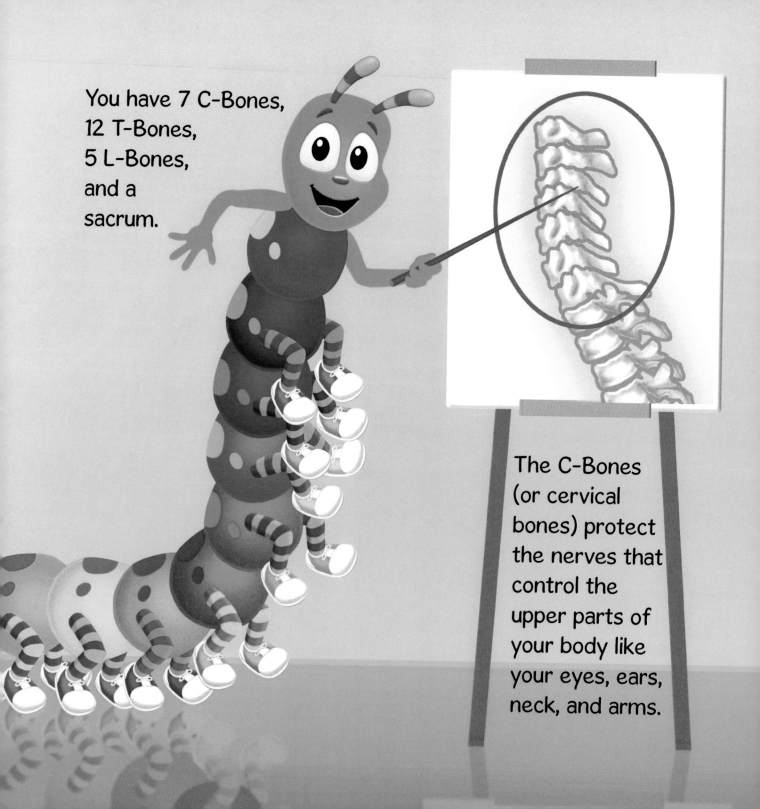

The T-Bones (or thoracic bones) are in the middle part of your spine.

These bones protect the nerves that control your heart, lungs and stomach.

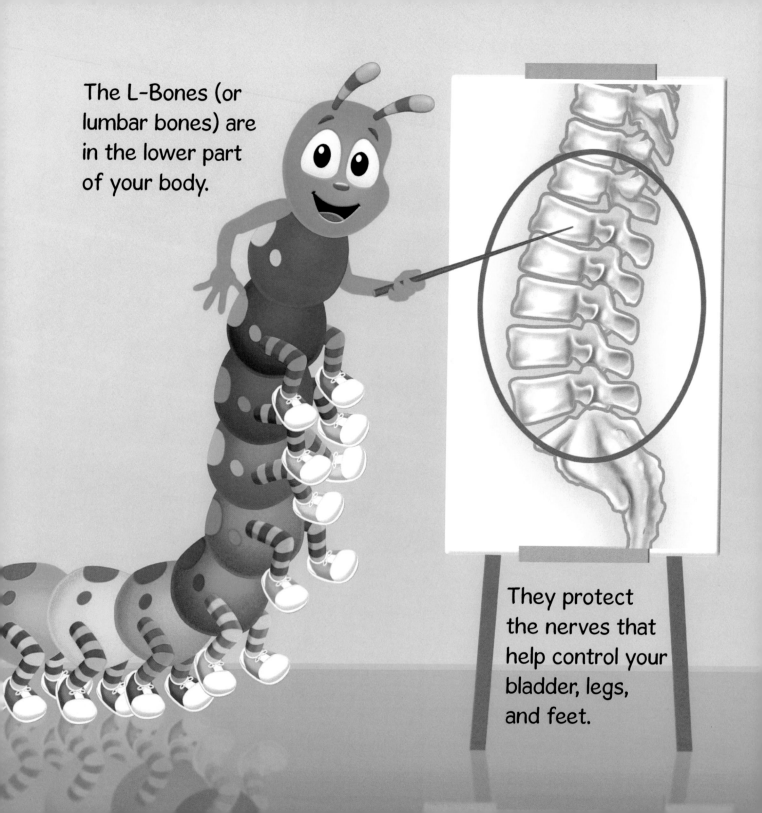

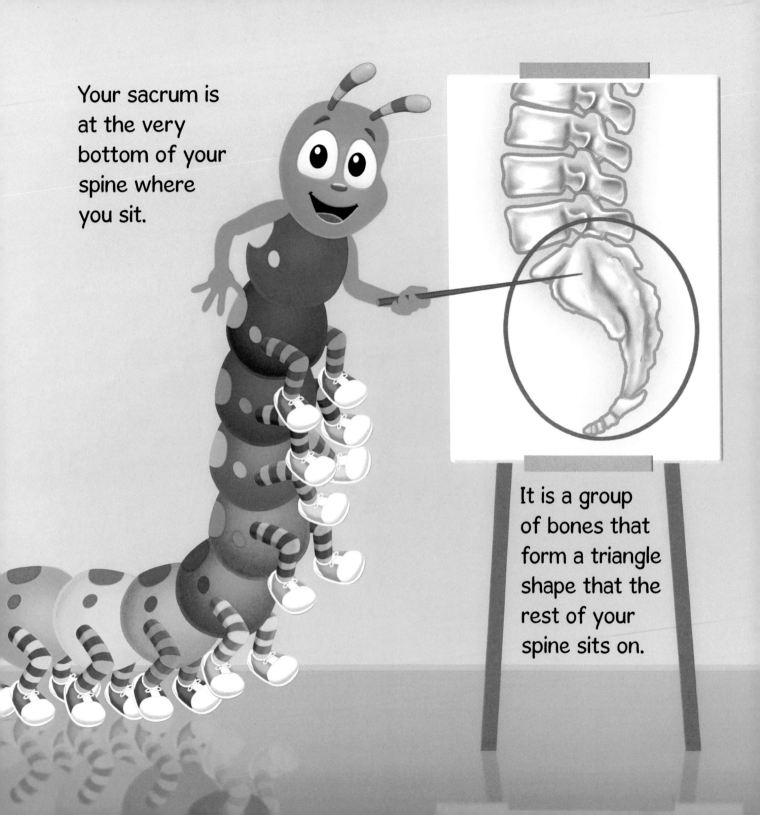

Each of the 24 bones in your spine were all made to move together in a certain way. When you fall or twist your body in a way that it is not used to, you may cause some of your spinal bones to move out of the right place. They will not be able to move like they should.

Your spine is not well when this happens, and your body may become sick or will not work as well as it could.

Your friend, the chiropractor, can give you an adjustment of your spine. An adjustment will help put your bones back in the right place. Then they will be able to help every part of your body feel its best.

You may do some checks that will be like playing a game of Simon Says. Your chiropractor may tell you to touch your toes, twist, or raise your legs up and down like a marching soldier.

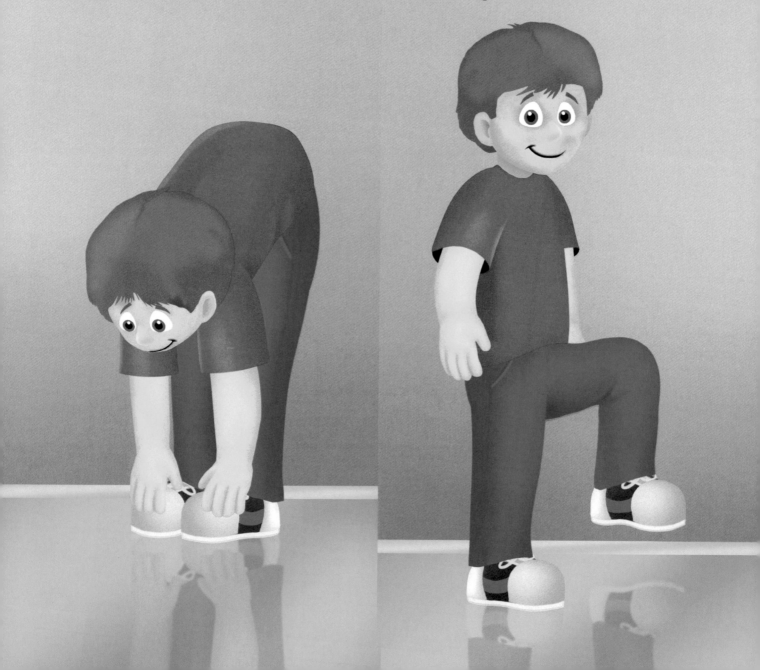

Another fun way your chiropractor may have you do checks is to have you climb aboard a padded table or bench. He or she may have you lie face down. Don't worry; there is a place for your nose!

Doing these checks is also a lot like playing Simon Says. Sounds like fun, doesn't it? The chiropractor will measure your legs after each of these checks to see if they are the same length. That is one way he or she will know if you need an adjustment.

If you need one, your chiropractor will give you an adjustment to put your spine back in line so it can work the best for you. An adjustment is given by a chiropractor like this: he or she will push down on different parts of your back with their hands, or they may use a funny looking gadget. There are many ways to adjust your spine. Your chiropractor will pick the right way to help your spine work better.

An adjustment doesn't take long. Chiropractic adjustments sometimes feel like a little push on your back. Once in awhile you may feel a bit of soreness for a short time when you have an adjustment. This feels like you just exercised. Best of all, your friend the chiropractor does not give shots or icky tasting medicine. To help your body heal, you should not play hard for a couple of hours. Then you'll be feeling great!

I've had fun visiting with you today and just remember:

A visit to your chiropractor
Will keep your spine in line
After an adjustment
You'll be feeling very fine!

Your friend,
Sammy the Centipede

Acknowledgments:

I would like to thank the following people in addition to my loving family for their encouragement, critique and support in the preparation of this book:

Claudia Anrig, D.C.
Dennis Dilday, D.C., who keeps my spine in line
Kathleen Eberle, Physical Therapist from Laumersheim, Germany

A special thanks to Thomas R. Hurst, D.C. for his excellent chiropractic care of my daughter, Tara, when she was a child. Chiropractic adjustments made it no longer necessary for her to take medication for asthma. This experience served as the inspiration for this book.

About the Author:

Maria Luchsinger is a teacher and literacy advocate who has a passion to write engaging and educational books for children.

She was awarded two scholarships on her way to graduating with honors from Central Washington University with a Bachelor of Arts in elementary education.

Contact Maria Luchsinger for more information as shown below:
Email: Maria@Marialuchsinger.com.
Twitter: @Marialuchsinger
Linked In: Maria Luchsinger
Facebook: Sammy the Centipede
Pinterest: Maria Luchsinger, Author

Other books by Maria include:

Sammy the Centipede Goes to the Chiropractor

by Maria Luchsinger

Illustrations by Joe Palmisano

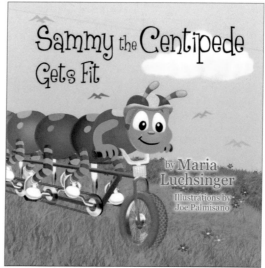

Sammy the Centipede Gets Fit

by Maria Luchsinger

Illustrations by Joe Palmisano

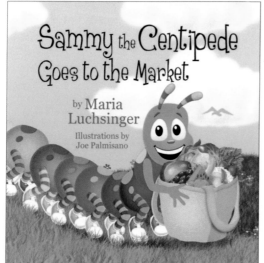

Sammy the Centipede Goes to the Market

by Maria Luchsinger

Illustrations by Joe Palmisano

Sammy the Centipede Goes to the Dentist

by Maria Luchsinger

Illustrations by Joe Palmisano

You will find
Sammy the Centipede books at
www.MariaLuchsinger.com

28183809R00018

Made in the USA
Columbia, SC
16 October 2018